To: Don and LaVerne,

— Our Love —

Because of His Love,

Ev, Liz, Larry

Aug. 1998

To thank Larry for any
special blessing received:
Mr. M.Lawrence Fuller
White Gables Lodge
8592 Lampson Ave
Garden Grove, CA 92641

Until the Shadows Flee Away

Poems of My Life

Morris Lawrence Fuller

Until the Shadows Flee Away

Poems From My Life

ISBN 1-57502-531-0

Printed in the USA by

MORRIS PUBLISHING

3212 East Highway 30 • Kearney, NE 68847 • 1-800-650-7888

Forward

Dear Larry,

Thank you for asking me to write a "Forward" to your book of poems. I count it a privilege. Bless you, Larry, in your new adventures. I pray that the best will work out for you.

Not many years ago Dr. Henri Nouwen wrote a classic book about Jesus called THE WOUNDED HEALER. The Old Testament prophet, Isaiah, has affirmed this when he wrote: "By His wounds we are healed," and the Apostle Paul, in the New Testament, bears witness: "For you know the Grace of our Lord Jesus Christ, that though He was rich, yet for your sakes He became poor, so that you through His poverty ... might become rich."

God calls all Christians to be "wounded healers," but in some ways there are people who are set apart by their disabilities to be special. Larry Fuller is one of these. His father—a physician—and his mother—a nurse—served as medical missionaries in Ecuador, Panama, Africa, and Israel, as well as in the United States.

Larry is the oldest of seven children. At age 21, he was diagnosed with schizophrenia. This was very hard for the whole family. But it was not long before they realized that God had given him an unusual gift to bless the heart of God, and be of encouragement to many. The gift is poetry. Out of his own woundedness Larry has been able to weave his life story in such a way that it ministers to others.

I first met the Fuller family in a little H.C.J.B. World Radio hospital in the midst of the Amazon jungles of Ecuador in the summer of 1955. To my delight, I became reacquainted with them in 1991, and since then have had the pleasure of reading many of Larry's poems. He faithfully shares his heart through tough as well as good times. I have sensed an unusual depth of intimacy with God. The Lord has blessed me as I've walked part of Larry's journey with him. I am sure you will feel God's healing as you read these words from a special "wounded servant of Jesus Christ."

> Sincerely,
> Rev. Donald M. Meekhof,
> Associate Pastor of Care and Healing,
> First Presbyterian Church, Spokane, Washington

Dedication

You Are Ready For His Banquet

E -ver I sing your praises, darling Mother,
L -ittle though, for now, we see each other.
I -n my heart you are the dearest ever—
S -weetest in your ways. May nothing sever!
A -bout your head may bounty bloom like flower;
B -elow in beauty may you make your bower!
E -ver may your love shine, by HIS POWER!
T -ill fades the earth... HOME comes, at last,
H -eaven's Joy shall fill ... at HIS REPAST!

— An Acrostic for Mom: For Love —

Acknowledgements

To my mother, Elisabeth Parsons Fuller, and to many dear friends, as well as less known acquaintances, who have said that they have sensed a spiritual uplift, and soul-encouragement, after enjoying just one of my many poems.

My sincere appreciation of and for Frances Riggs Vecchio ... for manuscript corrections. My mother knew of your twenty-five years as an English teacher at Lewis and Clark High School in Spokane. You rank very high in the memories of many students whom you instructed!

Special thanks to Morris Publishing for their availability, and for their fine personnel, who have answered questions as this manuscript has been assembled for this book ...

UNTIL THE SHADOWS FLEE AWAY
(poems of my life)

Preface

By Heaven's Design
(your mom)

First born son from mother's womb—
Joy of World War's baby boom—
Sacred gift from dad's fond love—
My first-born child from Heaven above.

You've been our joy amid your pain!
If we could run it o'er again
We'd leave it to His Great Design—
Nor change one plan of His ... for mine!

You've always been a special son!
Stay as you are ... 'til race is run.
Blessed be the tie that binds our hearts
With all the joy that God imparts!

... to Larry ...
our "forever" love

Your Dad and Mom

Section One

Until The Shadows Flee Away
Poems of my life

We're Blessed in Jesus, giving Him His Due
We follow on, from His: "SO SEND I YOU!"

Encouragement
Meditation
Reflection
Prayer
Praise

Morris Lawrence Fuller

INDEX

A Sonnet of Love For Jesus

Through lonely lands of hunger and of thirst,
Love-lorn and lost, I wandered in my sin;
With fettered bands were selfish habits cursed,
And tempest-tossed was oft' my soul within!

But then, a Way was found for vagrant feet.
A Truth was heard enlightening my path,
And a Blest Life was given—so replete
With Grace: Christ died and satisfied God's wrath!

With spirit welcoming You, Lord, to dwell,
And soul responding to Your Tender Care,
My ready mind has been prepared to tell
This word of joy I now to You declare.

Mine is the will to love You, Blessed One.
Your Mighty Love ... my lonely heart has won!

But Look To Jesus Lord And King

Go into the Mount of God
And take a higher view;
All changed will be the meaner sod,
And all life's carings, too.

Just give to God your earnest best,
To His Dear Will be turning;
He'll grant all power and all rest ...
Your heart with His be burning.

And trust the God of very Grace
For every sort of need.
Your wants with blessings He'll enlace,
With fruit grown from His Seed!

Just look to Jesus, Lord and King,
He'll touch your inward seeing;
Your thoughts and prayers will take to wing,
God's Law ... delight your being!

But Think Of Jesus And His Holy Cross

Dear Soul, perturbed by something of a loss,
Of ways awry, and different than before—
But think of Jesus and His Holy Cross,
Of bitter waves encumbering o'er and o'er!

His was a trial more severe than all,
Yet, He endured to see it to its end.
His pain was beckoning from the cradle stall;
His sorrows to our comfort, gladly lend.

His is the victory and He hails us still,
For all endeavor to be sound and strong;
He holds us in His Great and Holy Will,
'Til all our sorrows issue in a song!

He looks upon us with grieved and Glory Face,
And opens up the Treasures of His Grace!

From The Parapet Of Heaven

What would I *see*
If I were given to sit upon the parapet of Heaven
And look beyond and down below?

What would I *think*
As there I sat, my dangling feet precariously
Hung down … yet calmly sitting and secure?

What would I *feel*
If something more than abject silence
Met me through the deep deep air?

Ah! Who shall ever think or hear or feel
The way God does,
When, from the parapet of Heaven …

He Views *Our Little World?*

God Doesn't Give In Part

We give our gifts and in a certain measure,
Give of ourselves; a bond of love renewing.
God's greatest gift is of abundant treasure;
He gives in fully gracious "doing".

God gave His Son, the Father's Love imparted,
Draws wide the door for everyone's receiving
The Grace of Life; and to the tenderhearted,
A life in Grace is given, through believing.

God's Son gave all! His Love, our faith securing!
In Him is Life. In Him we have our being.
He gave His All! We love Him... without seeing!
His Life, in us, gives Life, past time, enduring!

God Is There

When we are at a loss for thought or speech,
When power is almost gone to stand or reach,
When things seem much too much to hold and bear,
God is STRENGTH, and He is THERE!

When days are dark, so that we lose our way,
When thoughts go scattered, and we'd rather stay ...
Though grip the burdens, even in the air,
God is LIGHT, and HE is THERE!

When night, so starless, is our way and lot,
When we're anguished for a thing that we have sought,
When things go tumbling down a hidden stair,
God is HELP, and HE is THERE!

When hope seems helpless ev'n to arouse a smile,
When seems we cannot go another mile;
When seems we've lost all comfort and all care,
God is LOVE and HE is THERE!

He Is Our Lord Of Steadfast Love

From Heaven Jesus came to dwell …
Our Great Lord God, IMMANUEL!
He took upon Himself our frame,
Maintaining His Own Glory-Name!

Jehovah-Jesus lived and died,
To open Mercy's Fountain wide!
The Shepherd bore away our sin;
The Lamb cleansed us, all whole within.

We come to Him, with sinful deed,
Find Grace to help our time of need.
He carries us in Mighty Arms,
And soothes away all our alarms.

He knows our lot; He feels and shares;
High Priestly Robe He ever wears …
And each … His children, gladly bears.

His Blessings pour from Heaven Above!
HE IS OUR LORD OF STEADFAST LOVE!

I Cry And Ask

I cry and ask, I search, and longing ... wait.
I think now is the day to firmly stand,
While many others pray to Heaven's gate,
As evil stalks throughout the land!
Is Romance-Blent-Reality my fate?

I think of Arthur and The Holy Grail;
Of Merlin-lore and knightly clash of swords.
Of Yesu-Masih: Lord Messiah, Hail!
Teach me Thy hope, and Amma's* Fire-Words—
Bold through the mist, and stalwart through the gale.

Three Hebrew Children were thrown into the fire—
Who would not bow to edict of the king.
Their faith was strong; unearthly, their desire,
Though die they must—while dying they would sing,
True-Faithful first—and mindless of all ire!

Three were thrown in; FOUR WALKED ROUND AND ROUND!
(They might as well have been on Heaven's Shore.)
No brand could burn! All raptured and unbound,
Jehovah's Righteousness they gladly wore,
And His Communion, in extremis, found!

Dear Lord, Return those days of Burning Hearts!
Life ... that's surely lived in Heaven Above;
When swept the field of all its fiery darts—
Sword of the Spirit, and Triumphant Love ...
Our God's Whole Armor, and All-Praying Arts.

*Amy Carmichael, Irish missionary to South India, prayed
that her words, in prose and poetry, be of HEAVENLY FIRE!

It's No Easy Road To Heaven Above

It's no easy road to Heaven above …
For Jesus calls disciples, "Come, and die."
A daily dying is what life is of;
All earnest praise forbids the coward's sigh,
As we press on in all the ways of Love.

Amid perplexities we pray for Light.
Let every burden weigh, we still will stand,
Upheld by our own Lord's so Blessed a Might;
Glad for His Promise, endeared to His Command,
By Grace and Faith, we follow on … to fight!

Not for the world's pleasures are we taught to stay,
Nor after other worldling's praise we go.
Far other is the Vision we obey;
Much other is the Truth we gladly know,
Upon the Lightsome and the Heavenly Way!

Sweet Rose of Sharon, blooming in our hearts,
Dear, Lovely Lord, we follow in Your Stead.
With all the blessings, Your Great Grace imparts,
From this world to the next, we're surely lead.

In Deepest Gratitude Our Praising Starts!

Jesus Calls Us To Be Strong

What now, Our Soul? Instead the battle waging,
Why linger on in all a vagrant loss?
Why not, all earnest, every foe engaging,
Stand true—till victory in the Mighty Cross?

Why listless now, to slip, and sink, and languish?
Another's warfare calls us now to scan.
His day is darkness, and increased His anguish.
Behold! Our Savior! Yes, Behold the Man!

Why turning from the conflict and fainthearted,
When underneath are everlasting arms?
Why not trust God for all His Grace imparted,
To meet, and conquer, all your known alarms?

Up! Up! Be strong and all the while enduring
To measure well and deeply count the cost.
The prize is there, and it is all alluring,
Amidst the lesser things that needs be lost!

Of Christian Faith And Love

We stand among the ranks of faith and fervor,
To trust in Jesus Christ, our Living Lord.
We rest on promises of Friend and Savior,
Who draws us forth with many a loving cord.

We've turned from dark into a Light, most Glorious!
We follow on … supported by The Word;
Our fight is with examples all victorious
We walk, by faith … our pathway, undeterred.

By this, we show our own glad believing—
Without a sight, but inward … sure and sweet!
How greatly dear, The Earnest, we're receiving …
'Til open-faced, Our Jesus, we shall greet!

What blessings ours, in simple trust obeying
Our Precious Lord, though seeing not … we love!
He bears, for now, all cares that we are laying,
Until we see Him, face to Face, ABOVE!

Of The Child In My Heart

Though through the years,
With many a broken place,
And sadness of my unshed tears,
Yet the blessings of God's Grace …

I have a crying and a prayer
To Him who's Mercy and is Just;
To Him do I repair desiring,
Though broken be my trust.

Praying, "Jesus, Do Thy Love impart,
To this SMALL CHILD who's in my heart!"

Of The Struggle With Delusion

O Lord, the waves upon me fall,
Against You, Savior, All in All!
I felt them once, in agony;
Now they return ... and tremblingly.

First sweep the waves of Very Christ;
All-Holy Word! Yet, warped and diced!
A passage here ... a passage there ...
So filling with unstable care!

O Jesus, Cure the mighty wrong,
That I may sing ... though Evensong!
In praise of Your Own Power and Grace,
While You, my lawlessness ... erase!

Oh! Feelings rise, and I confess
My pride and my unrighteousness!
Lord, sit with Your Refining Fire!
Purge, and Heal ... all heart's desire!

My pain is conscious, dark and deep.
Sometimes I cry ... ev'n in my sleep.
I pray, that this, a thorn of grief,
By Grace, BE GONE ... with Dear Relief!

I am not like Your Paul, of old,
With revelations making bold.
I have no Gospel ... but the same ...
With which to glorify Your Name!

On Providence

Thanks for Your Great All-seeing Eyes,
Our paths of life do all apprise
Out of so Good Your Righteousness—
And wondrously Your Faithfulness!

From childhood days unto our age ...
Despite the battles that we wage,
The Beacon of Your Light shines true,
Upon all ways that we pursue.

O Kindly Father, Gracious Son,
You'll always guide— 'til life is done!
You will, forever, to our days,
Be Blessed Guide, our Life, our Praise.

Thanks for Your Vision, so to bless;
Thanks for Your Spirit's Still Caress.
Thanks that You lead us on ... Above!
Thanks for the Foresight ... of Your Love!

Precious Is The Calm That Jesus Brings

Oh! How soothing is Love's Balm
    to our deep sufferings;
Oh! How precious is the calm
    that Jesus surely brings ...
When to the storm and wind ...
    "Be still!" He cries;
And to the one who's sinned ...
    "FORGIVEN! ARISE!"

Jesus is Lord of all, who, when
    in their distress,
Look, in faith, to Him, and call
    on His Great Faithfulness.
Lovingly, He hears the prayer,
    and calms the troubled breast;
Tenderly, He lifts each care.
    "Just come to Me ... and rest!"

Until The Shadows Flee

Man of Sorrows, grieved and slain,
My love—thoughts rouse and yet remain!
Frankincense, my praise and prayer
To You, O Lord, The Fairest Fair!

Until the shadows flee away,
Until the break of Heaven's Day,
Myrrh Mountain is a climb I'll gain;
A token of my Savior's pain!

> Myrrh is an aromatic gum resin
> From a tree found in Arabia,
> And East Africa, and this resin
> Exudes a bitter taste.

We Are All Pilgrims

We are all pilgrims on this long, long road
Out of ourselves, and to Thy Love, O God!
We journey earnest, with our souls afire,
And burning, in our hearts, but one desire!
Better and best, our pathway here to go;
Thy Love to other pilgrims, gladly show.

And pray ... It stays ... forever in our sight,
As we journey, earnest, toward Thy Heavenly Light.
How we long for nurtured ways within!
The touch of healing from our frequent sin!
O Teach us, Jesus, each new path to sense,
And Thy Great Mercy, Lord, to us dispense!

That one day we may hold Thy Precious Hand,
And by Thy Death ... our journey understand!
Teach us Thy Ways by little things of grace,
And lead us onward— 'til we see Thy Face!
NO LONGER PILGRIMS— traveling Earth's sand;
But then, Our God, ACCEPTED IN THY LAND!

We Seek Our Lord And Find Him

Oh! Well behold … a little candle in the dark,
A little promise meant for so much good!
Lift up your eyes, to wing, as would the lark;
Take bit by bit, a portion of your Daily Food.

"Seek Me, and you shall find!" 'Tis very Truth,
For older age, as well as tender youth.
God puts His Faithfulness to test,
As far as any East is … from the West!

We seek our God, and find Him! This, for sure!
We can all confident, in this promise rest.
His Word, FOREVER, will both STAY … ENDURE;
And we receive a portion with the Blest.

Wake up, O Soul, from hoary dark ... to Light;
For as You find ... You WILL RECEIVE YOUR SIGHT!

Section Two

It Is For You!

The Promise, settled, sure—
Of home in Heaven, waiting there before;
All formed and ready, ever to endure,
The prize of Hope for all that Jesus bore!

INDEX

A Bruised Reed Shall He Not Break

(Matthew 12:20)
(A poem for the mentally disabled)

I am a reed, much bruised, O Lord!
Yet, I am in Your Hand.
May I, with You, have glad accord—
A Tender, Loving Band.

O Lord, encircle with Your Grace
My lonely, saddened need!
And in Your Word, I'll see Your Face,
And be, for You... Your Reed!

You can make of me a flute,
And play our music round,
So Grace and Faith can have Good Fruit—
Where Love and Joy abound!

Send forth Judgement on ahead—
Ev'n to Your Victory …
Where All Bruised Reeds Be Healed and Led …
With Tunes Of Purity!

All Promise Of The Golden Store

You call us, Lord— no easy road to tread.
Yet point us where You've gone before.
We follow, and we fight in Your Own Stead,
Blest by all Promise of The Golden Store!

Alone, Dear Lord, we cannot even stand!
Yet, with Your Strength we shall all fervent go;
And You will lead us 'till Emmanuel's Land;
To Victors of The Faith we'll gladly know!

Oh! Lead us ... Lord, to follow and to fight
For all the Best that You, Yourself, design.
May Your Blest Ways be our own dear delight!
Your Love to spur us, Line on Gracious Line!

Courage! Dear, Dear Souls; fresh courage take,
To war; to fight, to wrestle, and to pray!
Jesus, Your Overcoming Victor, make.
He is Your Tower, Shield ... and Stay!

Come, Learn Of Me

(Matthew 11:29)

"Come, Learn of Me." "O Lord, I hear Your Voice!
No trembling message this— by shades of night!
Instead, it bids me, clearly, to rejoice;
That You will teach me! Lead me *IN THE LIGHT!"*

"Come, Learn of Me." "O Dear Lord, let Your Word
Sink deep within this troubled heart of mine …
That I may live from day to day, assured
Of Grace, through Faith … that needs *NO OUTWARD SIGN!"*

"Come, Learn of Me." In learning, Lord, I'll grow
In Faith and Grace! This is The Precious Fruit
Of Righteousness, I'll find, because I know
My Shepherd's Voice … and let His WORD take root!

Ecuadorian Memories

Dear Land, bathed by the Equatorial sun …
In fondest memories I once more return,
To climb your mountain heights … to nimbly run,
Along moist brooklet paths bedecked with fern.

I wake upon Pichincha's grassy slope
To watch the Southern Cross die with the night;
To take the eastern skies in sweeping scope;
As rosy streamers wend their wandering flight.

A darkened hillock path I walk along,
And stop enchanted—catching on the breeze
A mournful, piercing, melancholy song
That floats through pungent eucalyptus trees.

A hoary head of majesty I see;
Here … once proud Incas cried upon the sod,
"O Chimborazo, we do worship thee—
But praise your maker, if you be not God!"

In but a moment's reverie,
The years of life go swiftly flying by.
The past is gone! 'Tis just a memory …
But in my heart THE LAND WILL NEVER DIE!

      Pichincha … extinct volcano
      Chimborazo … 22,000 feet high extinct volcano

Dearest Jesus

O Dearest Jesus, Meek and Lowly,
With Your Meekness, make me holy!
I would burn with single flame
To honor, glorify Your Name.

Dearest Jesus, Great and Truthful,
I would, like You, truly be youthful!
True to serve and true to love …
As Your Heavenly Hosts Above!

Dearest Jesus, Sweet and Fervent,
Caring, Loving, Blessed Servant,
Teach me so to follow near,
That I, Your Precepts all hold dear!

Dearest Jesus, I'd be proving
All my love from sin, removing.
So may all my heart's desire
Be aflame with *HOLY FIRE!*

Eternal Lord On High- Our Guardian of Vows

Akin to vows, O God, are my earnest prayers!
In which I ask and claim Thy Mighty Power;
Encounter Thee ... as deep confession bares
My heart, as best I can ... in solemn hour!

Be pleased, Lord, to forgive and cleanse and heal
With Tender Grace, upon my sore, sore needs.
Who, but to Thee can one approach ... appeal
For All Thy Great and Blessed Saving-Deeds?

I do, in various ways, repeat my cries;
Oh! May they not come vain into Thine ears!
Still, and yet more, my heart unto Thee flies,
Out of the woe-begone and deeply troubled years.

Dear God! Eternal Guardian of my vows,
To Thee, and to Thy Grace, I do apply,
Whole-heartedly, within, my being bows,
To call, and claim Thee: SAVIOR LORD ON HIGH!

From Cross To Crown Eternal Gain

All through the darkening world,
Deep-darker draws the age;
Yet more Love's Banner is unfurled
From out The Sacred Page.

The Lamb's own Bride Herself prepares,
Adorning grace-on-grace.
His Likeness all the more She wears—
Yet ... longs to see His Face.

Oh! Dear the cost of Bridal Love,
To count self's baubles loss;
Keep dwelling with our hearts Above,
Keep joying in His Cross!

What though His Cross to mortal pain
Is of the path we go?
From Cross to Crown ... ETERNAL GAIN
Is what God's Martyrs know!

Jesus, Keep Our Love ... Oh! Keep it Burning

Lawlessness is filling all our land,
And evil-dark are much the days we scan!
We need to heed our Lord's so dear Command:
Be faithful woman; and be faithful man.

We follow Jesus with Love's great desire;
Unselfish burning in our heart-of-hearts
From Him and to Him burns Love's dauntless Fire;
From His Own Grace, our holy praising starts!

May we be so filled ... we overflow,
With God's Great Spirit, from His Home Above;
That Holiness in fragrant spices blow,
From our heart's garden, to the Lord we love!

O Jesus, keep our love; O keep it burning—
To dwell, yet deeper in Your Will!
And, fix our all on You, with tender yearning,
Glad-taught, Love's Yielding ... Sure and Still!

Lord, I Need You Ere
The Fight Begins

My Lord, I need You ere the fight begins—
In quiet know Your Spirit's Holy Power!
Consume my dross and cleanse within;
Do all I can't, in Your Own Godly Hour ...
Your Triumph over lust and over sin!

Press me, Lord, into Your Service, Dear!
Teach me, Master, of Your Work and Word.
Lead me, God, into a holy fear.
Aid my faith ... that You will undergird!

Grant me, Creator, certain special wings
For Spirit-flight and for this sober war!
(Though such request not come to You before)
Upon Your Word my heart all surely clings.

So like on eagle's pinions I may mount ... *
To endless skies of azure, gray, or black;
And gaze on Glory- LIFE'S ETERNAL FOUNT!
There drink; desire; yet, drink and never lack!

Oh! Teach me, Spirit ... Brooding on the deep,
Upon the waters; or ... soaring Heaven's Steep!

> *Isaiah 40:31 "But those who wait upon the
> Lord, shall renew their strength; they shall
> mount up with wings ... like eagles ... ."

Lord Jesus Christ Search Deep In Me

Dear Lord, I find mixed is my heart's desire.
Refine the gold. Purge out my selfish dross.
Search deep in me! Your Holy, Heavenly Fire—
Mark all I am with Your All-Conquering Cross!

Sometimes I feel I'm so much swept about—
I ride Your Sea, and yet, I pitch and toss.
"Oh! You of little faith! Why do you doubt?"
"Speak, Lord! Through quickening of Your Cross!"

For me, the Dear, and Great Emmanuel died!
My Hallelujas ... to The Crucified!

How easily to vain pursuits I tend;
Lord Jesus, all such gain, let it be loss.
May I to Your Sweet Will, all gladly bend;
Draw me to love You In Your Holy Cross!

Memento Mori*

1st Corinthians 15:51-57

Lord Jesus … What of my deathly pain?
For day or night will come when I must go!
Oh! May it be in victory I had lain,
Well taught … humility to show!

When come the hours, or days, or years to wait,
When pain fast closes in this human breast,
May I be readied to enter Heaven's Gate,
To go … with other Christians into rest!

Old Death, You die! When Jesus claims His Bride!
For those who die in Christ are just to rise!
Then … all remaining, go through open skies,
Transformed Forever! All That's DEATH Defied!

We shall be changed! In twinkling of an eye
All wrinkle, and all blemish gone away.
The Glory of His Likeness … come to stay!
No more of pain! NO MORE TO GRIEVE OR DIE!

*From the Latin: "Remember, You Must Die."

My Jesus, Yet I Call You Blest

My Jesus, with the thoughts that wing and throng,
I find I am so often beating air!
Lord! Lessen vanity! How long … How long!
Dark Lion's pride resists a Contrite Prayer.

Would I could be all open-faced with You!
Confess my ways … though I be SO DISTRESSED!
Above my Gray is Your Supernal Blue.
I live in twilight … * yet I call YOU BLEST!

> *First Corinthians 13:12 says: What we see now is like a dim image
> in a mirror; then, we shall see Face to Face.

Panamanian Sunset

As another day is finished,
As the working hours are done,
All the heavens show God's Glory
At the setting of the sun.

As the radiant sphere goes sinking,
Slowly sinking 'neath my view,
Lord, I see Thy Finger Painting,
Etching color on the blue.

As the clouds are bathed in crimson
All along the evening west,
I can only love and praise Thee,
And in Thee find peace and rest.

Praise The Lord For Tender Ways And True

We all have need of God's Own Great, Great Grace
That He pours out into our mind and heart;
And He has so blessed those of the human race,
With every blessing which He does impart!

He touches us through His most Precious Word;
Through many a promise, and many a good command.
He, faithfully, sets Himself … to undergird …
That we may trust, and by Him … *UNDERSTAND!*

Praise be the Lord … for Tender Ways and True!
Praise be the Lord … for Goodness and for Love!
That we may live, and give to Him *HIS DUE*—
To worship … *HERE*; and wait for more … *ABOVE!*

Prayer Of Aspiration And For Healing

O God, great is my deep and fond desire
To live, alone, for Thee!
Cleanse me with Pure and Sacred Fire
In every part of me!

Heal, Lord! O Heal, where voices so molest
And work their wicked ill!
Then, grant unto my spirit Thy Own Rest ...
So amply Good and Still!

Prayer For Restoration

Quicken, Dear Lord, what You of Good began!
My First Love ... in days of hearty youth,
Before the course of illness ran;
When I, so dearly knew and practiced Truth.

'Twas then, Dear Lord, Your Will I gladly sought,
And I was on the path of "Shepherd Ways",
To preach and teach what You, in Grace, had wrought;
To live to honor You, with Love and Praise.

O Lord, How far, now, are those days behind!
I hesitate to ask You to restore.
And still, how close the vanities of mind!
The downward pull of some romantic lore.

Dear Lord, I pray ... Oh! Heal me all within!
Teach me to run, to strive, to fight!
Remove far from me all of lust and sin,
To walk along, with You ... *in HOLY LIGHT!*

So Surge On Forward, O My Soul

Like the great ocean roll on roll
So surge on forward, O my Soul!
Though tempests come, and wild waves toss
'Tis but a portion of Thy Cross.

Yet, after tempest, then comes calm;
And for my Soul, the Healing Balm.
Wind over wind ... sail on, *ALONE,*
'Till beckoned, I arrive ... AT HOME!

The Wonder Of God's Mighty Love

It is good, yes, so good … to have Faith in the Lord!
Faith in the Plenty, and the Good of His Word.
He is so wondrous, His Works to perform;
He walks on the wind; He rides on the storm!
He does all He does in The Wonder of Love.
He seeks us and saves us … that we rise Above!

Out of the marvel of Mercies, *UNTOLD*,
Streams forth the Blessings … that as they unfold
They pour down their sweetness of Heavenly Grace,
From God's Fullness of Love, and His Glorious Face!
We catch the Radiance that streams … from ABOVE …
And … *WE SHALL KNOW HEAVEN, THROUGH HIS
    MIGHTY LOVE!*

There Is A Lifting Up

Job 22:29

Sometimes our bark with sorrows tempest tossed,
A hearty labor has its purpose crossed;
Yet Jesus gives His gifts without alloy;
There is a lifting up … He comes with *JOY!*

Sometimes we're filled with earthly, fleshly care,
And can but hardly voice our needs in prayer.
Yet, Jesus' Promise is for all life's length!
There Is a lifting up … He comes, with *STRENGTH.*

Sometimes the billows mount, the burdens weigh,
The night is starless, and dark is the day;
Yet, Jesus sends His Spirit's Sweet Release;
There is a lifting up ... He comes with *PEACE.*

Sometimes our powers are low, with many a sigh,
And we are weary, tempted— wondering why?
Yet Jesus shows to Faith God's Glory-Face;
There is a lifting up … He comes with *GRACE!*

Sometimes we yearn to be all caught away;
Desire transfigured in Eternal Day;
Oh! Jesus bears us here toward Heaven Above,
There is a lifting up … *HE COMES WITH LOVE!*

Section Three

Life's Road

There is a road we all must take,
Though hard and long it be.
There is a race that must be run
To win … THE VICTORY!

INDEX

A Call To High and Heavenly Goals

The call goes out for stalwart souls
Who know and count the cost;
Who take to High and Heavenly Goals,
No matter tempest tossed.

No wind or storm can bar the way,
For such as go with God.
He is their Joy, their Song, their Stay;
They run ... or else they plod.

Up hoary heights, or down the vales,
All earnest take the road—
With trust in Him who never fails ...
Of Mercies so bestowed!

Oh! Seekers, follow Him today,
Whose blessings tend forever.
We owe our Jesus Sovereign Sway;
From Him, there's nought can sever!

A Prayer For Strength And Steady Watchfulness

Lord, give us stronger hearts,
Your purpose to pursue
With all that Grace imparts
For all we say and do.

Teach us to steady go,
Your paths of Right to take;
Your Loving kindness know,
Your Promise, ours to make.

Our days go on their round—
Complete the tale of years;
May nought in them be found
Of any selfish tears!

May we all watchful be—
Our wills bent for Your Best ...
'Till Jesus' Face we see,
And in His Presence rest.

As Moon Sheds Down to Earth Its Night-Tide Light

As moon reflects the glory of the sun,
So each of us a Lighthouse for the Lord—
Empowering each his pathway's race to run
Our Timeless Light—His faithful, precious Word.

We follow in Christ's footsteps all the way,
Supported by each promise that He gives;
Inspired by faith to gladly say,
"Praise be to God! In me, He surely lives!"

We have our little rounds of sense and time
In tune with God, our Great and Mighty Love.
We Join our wills with His in tender rhyme,
To sing His Praise, and blend with Hosts above.

As moon sheds down to earth its night-tide light,
May we, all gladly, be a *LIGHTHOUSE BRIGHT!*

Behold Him Who Is Our Heart's Desire

Ah! Paradise, of days without end!
Of zephyrs that yon glories ever send!
Of turns in timelessness all set to song,
And nevermore the blight of sin and wrong!

Our friends and family there we'll gladly greet,
Around the Dear and Memoried Mercy-Seat.
We'll bless the Savior, for our part with Him,
Amidst the Heavenly Throng of Cherubim!

Glad ministers of God's Own Will and Way …
To teach us more of Grace in Heaven's Day.
Wing, too, about Jerusalem, Above,
Where all is tuned to Praise and Perfect Love!

Yes, PERFECT LOVE, with all our hearts afire,
Beholding HIM, WHO IS OUR HEART'S DESIRE!

Blessed Be The Lord

Blessed be the Lord Most High—
Who has our heart so nourished!
He hears us at our slightest cry
And has our pathway flourished.

Blessed be the Lord, our Rock!
We're safe within His keeping.
He folds us with His tender flock
And holds us from our weeping.

Blessed be the Lord, our God!
He is so Tender-Hearted!
So sound His Praises all abroad
For all He has imparted.

Blessed be the Lord-of-All!
He has His Grace so splendid.
He blesses all this earthly ball,
His Love is never ended!

Come Our Beloved

The Lamb and we, His waiting Bride
Are parted but for short-a-time;
We're nearly at His Waiting Side
For everlasting life … SUBLIME!
The Father waits the Ransomed Sum;
The Spirit and the Bride say, "Come!"
"Come", is our prayer; yes, "Come, O Lord,
Our Savior, Lover, All-adored!"
Be it with Water, or with Fire …
"Come, Our Beloved, Our Desire!"

I Pray In My Pilgrimage

Sometimes in my anguish,
Sometimes in my loss—
Sometimes I'm appealing
To Christ and His Cross!

I ask in my pilgrimage—
Not yet … complete,
For Rest, in my Savior,
And Joy, at His Feet!

I Think Upon The Great-Souled God

Blessed be the God of all creation,
Who into primal dark spoke His Own Light!
Gave Love to be the dearest celebration,
Sent out His Son—Eternal Loving Right.

Before the starry hosts had bounds appointed,
Before God breathed in Adam living breath,
High Priestly Jesus had His Work anointed!
The Lamb was given for His Life-Giving death.

Oh! Glory of the Grace of God abounding,
To reach the deepest of a creature's sin!
Praise to the Highest ever be resounding,
For all Christ did to make us whole within!

With dear, dear joy our hearts are filled … o'erflowing,
To think upon God's magnanimity!
Great-Soul, He is … beyond our frailest knowing—
All-animating, Choice, Blest Trinity!

Look Look Ahead ...
Your Promised Goal

Wait on the Lord, though burning trial of fire
Be felt throughout The Vessel He Perfected.
Your lot and yearning for release, He knows.
He's planned Your Peace; and *YOU ARE NOT NEGLECTED!*

Wait on the Lord, though trials of sorrow loose
The throbbing fountains of the Deep.
Your tears may flow, today; but you shall know tomorrow,
In God's Home, *NO CHILDREN NEED TO WEEP!*

Wait on the Lord, though lengthy trials of Night
Beset your soul, and languid TIME prolongs.
Fear not! The cycling hours will ever bring
The breaking dawn, and birds awakening songs!

Wait on the Lord ... and hold your Pilgrim pace!
Trust in His Word with Faith's uplifted Face.
And be assured that as you run Life's race,
Through every trial, *HE'LL GIVE SUFFICIENT GRACE!*

Wait on the Lord, though tempests toss your Ship;
And mounting waves so buffet Limb and Soul!
Your *CAPTAIN* points ahead, and fearless, *SHOUTS,*
"LOOK! LOOK! AHEAD... YOUR PROMISED GOAL!"

O My Soul, Go To God

O my soul, go to God when all around, about,
Fall and roar the angry storms of doubt!
Seek Him who is your strength and refuge sure;
And find in Him, the Peace that will endure!

O my soul, go to God when sad at heart,
When hope seems gone, and all your joys depart!
Behold! Your Father stands with open arms
To wipe away all tears and guard from all alarms.

O my soul, go to God when trials rise,
When gloom hangs low, and darkened are the skies!
Be still and know that He, your Lord, is there,
And that He keeps you safe, within His Care!

O my soul, go to God when death is near!
Speak to Him then; His voice you soon will hear.
For 'tis but a moment, and you'll see His Face,
Who saved you by His Precious Love and Grace!

Our God Rules Over All

O Man, You have your little say,
To boast and proudly claim!
God has his Mighty Sovereign Sway—
THE POWER OF HIS NAME!

Man speaks and thinks to say so much,
In his, but transient hour!
So mindless of Almighty Touch;
(The clothing of a flower!)

Poor Foolish Man! Who thinks your words
Sweep all the globe around?
How does the earth, God undergirds,
Hang in her space, and bound?

So, You, of but a little dust,
Return … and praise the Lord!
The Savior of the humble just—
Ere He gird on His Sword!

Your pride will He to ground lay low!
Your works all come to nought!
The upright in God's Zion grow …
By Holy Spirit taught!

He stoops to lift the lowly up,
With Him to live and reign;
God is their portion and their cup
Who join His Heavenly Train!

Some Loves Grow Cold, While Others Blend With Joy

This is the hour when hearts that once were true,
Love more the worldly than their own Dear Lord.
Oh! well they may retain their church and pew—
Yet, Love ... grown cold ... minds not the Spirit's Sword.

So, bit by bit, they slow, and fall away—
Until they hear no more the Still, Small Voice;
Nor hear their Jesus, Captain, Rock, and Stay;
While there's much cause, enraptured, to rejoice!

Heavenly, Holy Spirit, Come and Brood,
As once, long ago ... on darkened deep!
May all true Children of Thy Day, endued,
Wing up! What though the chasm — hoar and steep!

Dear Spirit of The Lamb, and of The Bride,
Cry in our hearts: "Our Lovely Lord, Oh! Come."
May Joy, yet more and evermore abide,
While Grace and Faith bring in their Harvest Sum!

That We May Know What Is The Height And Depth And Breadth And Length

(Ephesians 3:18)

Climb valiant for the Heavenly Height—
All zealous, faithful, stirred;
To take each step in God's Good Light,
Supported by His Word.

Plumb down the ways of Wisdom's Deep—
God's Promises are sure!
He gives, in His Beloved's sleep;
His Grace and Peace endure.

God's Good Commands are very broad.
By them He does surround us.
We, patient run, and walk, and plod,
His Mercies bless and ground us.

We go along all of life's length,
God has so greatly blessed us!
As is our day … so is His Strength,
With hope and joy to rest us!

Sweet Paradise ... All Saints Eternal Home

Oh! Joy that Jesus Christ is risen from the dead!
Become the First-Fruits of all them that sleep.
Dear Church, for You He is Your Glorious Head,
And lasting comfort for all those who weep.

As to the dying thief, our Jesus cried—
(The first of saints to open Paradise)
To deal the Death-Blow, to Old Death He died;
Dear Eternal Life is ours! He, too, did rise!

Sweet Paradise ... All Saints' Eternal Home ...
From there, Oh! Never more TO THINK TO ROAM!

The Garden Of My Soul

Holy Gardener of my lonely soul,
Though weed and thorn have taken toll in enervating ways ...
Still, by Your Presence, Precious Grace,
I will my given place on earth adorn,
In blossoms for Your Praise!

But where, I wonder, ARE YOU, O my GOD?
Bereft I seem to stand upon the earth,
And know a weighted deep-borne dearth of light.
I do not understand my lengthened plight
Of fears by day, and languishing by night.

Thick, overhanging boughs have grown above me,
And even have obscured the quickening sun.
But still I know when present trial of faith is done;
The fruit of toil and tears will, in Your Sight ...
Be a great joy, and to my heart ... delight!

Thinking Compassionately Of Others

How soothing is Love's Balm
To our deep sufferings!
How precious is the calm,
That Jesus surely brings!

When, to the storms and winds,
His "Peace Be Still", He cries;
And to the one who's sinned ...
"YOU ARE FORGIVEN! ARISE!"

Thoughts On John 3:16

Why *"God so loved the world"*
　　is a deep mystery;
For Love's Banner was unfurled
　　by night, at Calvary.

"He gave" from His Great Heart in Heav'n
　　to ours … His Grace so free;
But to His Son, with grief, was giv'n
　　the price of agony.

God's Holiness inviolable,
　　demanded justice done
In punishment deniable
　　to all … save *His Own Son!*

The "Whosoever", we have heard.
　　Our wills will make the choice;
With Faith's glad "yes", to God's Good Word,
　　In Christ, we now rejoice!

We *"shall not perish,"* Praise His Name!
　　There is no fear of doom;
For He, who died is, yes, the Same,
　　Who lives in our heart's room!

Blest *"everlasting life"* will be
　　Our Father's Gift of Love—
Received through Jesus' Guarantee,
　　And sealed by Heaven's Dove!

To The Trinity Be Praise

Triune Shepherd of my soul,
Holy God ... I, You, extol!
Lord, my heart cries out in me,
"Blest are You ... eternally!"

Blessed Father, Glorious Grace,
Have You given the human race.
Unto You my praises be,
Now ... and everlastingly!

Blessed Son, Lord Jesus Christ,
Your Life's Blood for me sufficed!
Covering all my guilt and shame,
Hallowed! Hallowed! be Your Name!

Blessed Spirit, by Your Gifts,
From my soul all sorrow lifts.
Hopeful quiet my heart knows,
And to You ... my cup o'erflows!

Father, Dear and Sacred One,
Tender, Loving, Gracious Son,
Spirit, Kind in all Your Ways—
TO THE TRINITY BE PRAISE!

What Is It To Honor The Lord?

To honor the Lord is to love Him,
His precepts ... to obey;
To seek Him, and to own Him
As Lord, upon our way.

To honor the Lord is to love Him;
In Him we find our rest.
To trust Him is to give Him
His Way within our breast.

To honor the Lord is to love Him,
And give Him of our praise;
To speak of Him to others,
In our nights and in our days.

To honor the Lord is to love Him ...
To praise His Holy Name;
Our Guardian, and our Fortress,
Forevermore ... THE SAME!

Of My World Sorrow And A Heavenly Joy
(epic)

O Lord, Come near with Presence and with Power!
How I long … I might be near to You!
My heart's Delight, my Fortress, and my Tower;
My Blessed God … *YOUR GLORY BE MY DUE!*

Of My World Sorrow And A Heavenly Joy

Oh! I have drunk the dregs of world-sorrow;
Of things all past, and present, and to come;
Yet less, would I of sentient trouble borrow—
Romantic grief of many a tear, the sum!

Dear Ecuador, where deep my sadness started;
To hear the music of folkloric pain;
And to my tender soul so dear imparted ...
Came on an empathetic sort of gain.

I listened, somewhat rapt in sweet sensation—
To count my own tears, "in music", shed;
For all the broken of an Indian nation*
Such bitter-sweet a melancholy bred!

I was a tyro; but ... at the beginning
Of spirit word, as well as spirit deed—
Deep to deep taught; together, bent the pinning
Of good and ill ... the settled, vital seed!

Early on—was I pressed to the duty—
Too young for what maturity would do;
Yet, here and there, I did approve the beauty
Of Law and Promise; Grace and Covenant, too.

It seems too much I did, I did too young; becoming
Much too old, while still in tender youth!
It meant a certain, rueful, sad benumbing ...
Ev'n while so caringly I sought the Truth.

O Grief, that good to ill should be a-turning!
And yet, Dear Love of God has seen me through.
I'm the more bent to His Love—with yearning ...
Glad, in His Grace and Mercy—ever new!

Some, there are, who at an early age,
With faith and zeal preach His Holy Word;
Who take to heart full many a sacred page,
And find their God to seal and undergird.

I thought me such to give to God *my all*;
Sought Love to burn within my very heart;
Desired, for my Lord, to be in thrall;*
As passionate Mary chose the better part.

While I much longed that my love flourish—
Prayed that it fill my being through and through—
Yearned that Love's Way I gladly cherish—
Oh! Woe is me ... that pain should so ensue!

Yet I lived on ... despite the grief and anguish;
The pain but seemed to double up the love.
I loved the more, although I slipped to languish,
I prayed for Fiery Spirit from Heaven Above.

Then ... to the land of Panama invited ...
I gave my all to love, to serve, to care!
Yet, all in all, I found my spirit blighted
By animist milieu, too dear to bear.

I did what best I could of burden-bearing;
Yet, as a novice, taking on too much!

I found my being so entirely wearing
By darkened spirits—with dark touch on touch.

I sat upon a hill while overviewing
The far horizons down to eastern sea;
Such pensive thought to be all up and doing—
What dear evangel so devolved on me!

So great and sweet for me the ample vision;
With passion love to serve my Kingly Lord!
Yet, such demand on heart and soul my mission …
I was *too young* to bear the Spirit-Sword!

*A state of complete absorption

And so I went full many a saint to follow;
Their deep desires I wished could be my own.
I prayed almost to an anguish, God would hallow
Good Seed of Faith, in His Choice Garden sown!

Dear fragrant saints with testimony blowing;
The incense of their lives wafted high!
With Fruit of Spirit-virtues sweetly flowing …
And eagle pinions 'taught by God' … to fly.

Upon the mission field—so deeply stirring …
My heart leaped up to follow in the stead
Of many an example of faith and love enduring—
By the TRUE FAITH and LOVE of JESUS led!

And then, I thought of 'mystic sweet communion'.
With such a cloud of witnesses before—
With whom I'd share a dear and God-wrought union;
The Joys of all Gracious, Heavenly lore!

• • • •

It's hard to tell when psychic ill got started;
Yet, sad to say ... I see it, in the good!
Fervent ideal, from the real, was parted;
Betwixt deep grief and ample joys ... I STOOD!

•   •   •   •

Then... two good years at Houghton College* spending,
All gladly to the pastorate I prepared.
Whole being to my Bible studies bending;
In each and all, how happily I fared!

So sweet it was both here, and there, a-preaching;
My gladdened heart to share the Holy Word!
For faith and practice giv'n to the teaching—
By sensitive professors ... dearly stirred!

•   •   •   •

*Houghton is a Christian Liberal Arts College in N.Y. State.
I completed a Bible Major there. In my third year I started
to have mental problems in thought and behavior, which led
to my first of many breakdowns.

Oh! My Dear God, what woe came on ... while yearning
For You to be my soulful, hearty best!
What self-sought ways, instead of Holy Burning—
What turns of passion which *COULD NOT BE BLESSED!*

So many a saint's example truly given!
Was it in pride I sought their spirit near?
With my own spirit seeking Holy Heaven—
Oh! Was it thus I dropped so many a tear?

My world-sorrow swept my heart away.
The Good I prayed seemed so to turn to dust!
Repeated grief made dull both night and day,
Ev'n while I sought the Dear and Holy Just.

•   •   •   •

Lord Christ, transfigure my deep a melancholy
Of tears that last the whole of some nights through;
Oh! Turn from me what is romantic folly—
Exchanged for Joy and Love … each morning new!

Gracious God, I pray You bless my thinking—
So that it be of You my dearest thought!
From Your Sure Lessons may I not be shrinking;
Instead … all gladly be … one, *Spirit-taught!*

I weary, Lord, from out my sorrows turning—
When I would rather be a saint at rest;
With all my heart be really set to yearning
FOR YOU! My Heart's Ease, and my Savior Blest!

I've had the deeps of grief to so much spend me!
Oh! Now I pray a joyful peace within.
With Your Dear Word, the more and more, to tend me,
And Your Dear Wooing, my saddened soul … to win!

Come, Sweet Jesus! May I be more harkened
To Your Blest Word, and Over-arching Will.
With less a grief and dulness ... or a darkening,
So may my soul, in joy, rest and be still!

O Joy, You lift my head when I'm in weakness;
You turn my gaze, by faith, unto Your Face!
You teach me of Your Own Almighty Meekness,
And grant to me, rejoicingly, Your Grace!

Sweet Joy is Yours to give the tender-hearted;
You wend them high—and even to Your Throne!
Well-kept, in Tender Mercies; never parted …
Are they who are the Lamb's Own, Very Own!

Sometimes sweet sorrow blends with Heavenly Joys—
(For all of melancholy is not wrong)—
The evening's dusk of day, and night's alloys;
O God, You may impart *DEAR MIDNIGHT SONG!*

With Your so great and Providential Ways,
You do make glad the Family of Man.
It is a joy supreme ... Your Wonders scan.
"To You, O Great Jehovah-Jireh*, PRAISE!

   *Translated: "God will Provide"

Dear Heavenly Father, thanks for thus conceiving
A plan of Love-for-Joy ... to us come down!
What wondrous ways of Grace and Faith the weaving—
With You, The Weaver, and Your Christ ... to crown!

O Jesus, thank You for Your Joy, so given;
So availing... to dispel our night!
How wondrously You point us to Your Heaven—
For Joys Eternal that will burst upon our sight!

Most Holy, Heavenly Spirit, thank You for Wooing
The children-of-the-night ... into *Your Day!*
Thanks, thanks, for all Your Tender, Gracious Doing.
To Your Alluring, *may I NEVER TELL YOU, "NAY!"*